WE LOVE OUR DADDY

Published by:
Violet Life Publishing, A division of
I AM Possible Enterprise, LLC
P.O. Box 5161
Fairlawn, OH 44334

Email: Kennethjsmith@iampossibleenterprise.com
Website: iampossibleenterprise.com

Copyright 2021 by Kenneth J. Smith

Hardcover ISBN: 978-1-967081-38-7
Paperback ISBN: 979-8-9853254-2-3

All rights reserved. NO part of this book may be used, reproduced or transmitted in any form or by any means, electronic or mechanical, including photocopying and recording, or by any information storage and retrieval system without written permission from the publisher, except by a reviewer who wishes to quote brief excerpts in connection with a review in a newspaper, magazine or electronic publication. Requests for permission should be addressed in writing to:

I AM Possible Enterprise, LLC
P.O. Box 5161
Fairlawn, OH 44334

DADDY is very important and special to us.

When WE wake up in the morning DADDY cooks us breakfast. His oatmeal is the best, but WE like scrambled eggs and toast better than the rest. Don't forget the cheese!

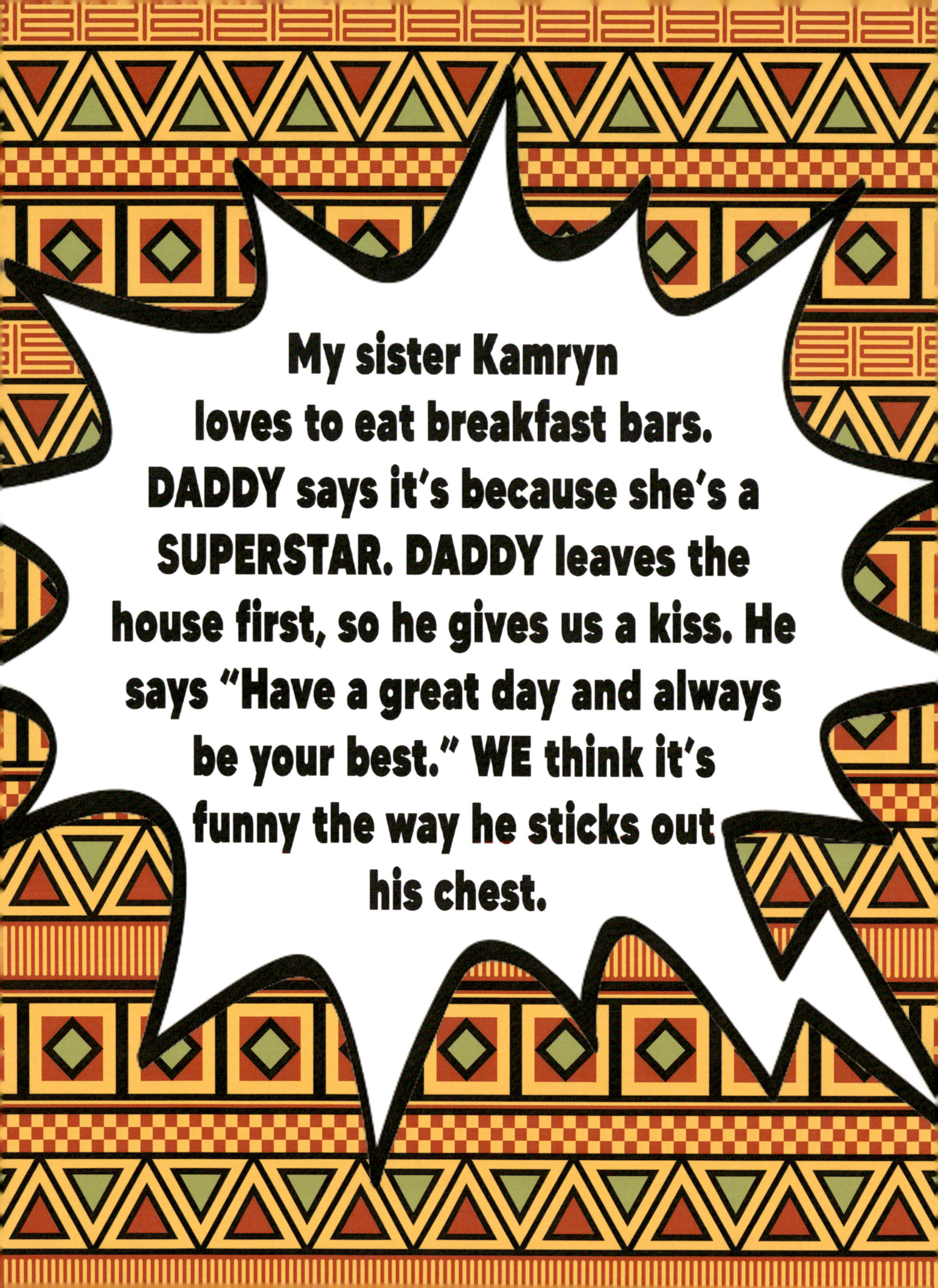

My sister Kamryn loves to eat breakfast bars. DADDY says it's because she's a SUPERSTAR. DADDY leaves the house first, so he gives us a kiss. He says "Have a great day and always be your best." WE think it's funny the way he sticks out his chest.

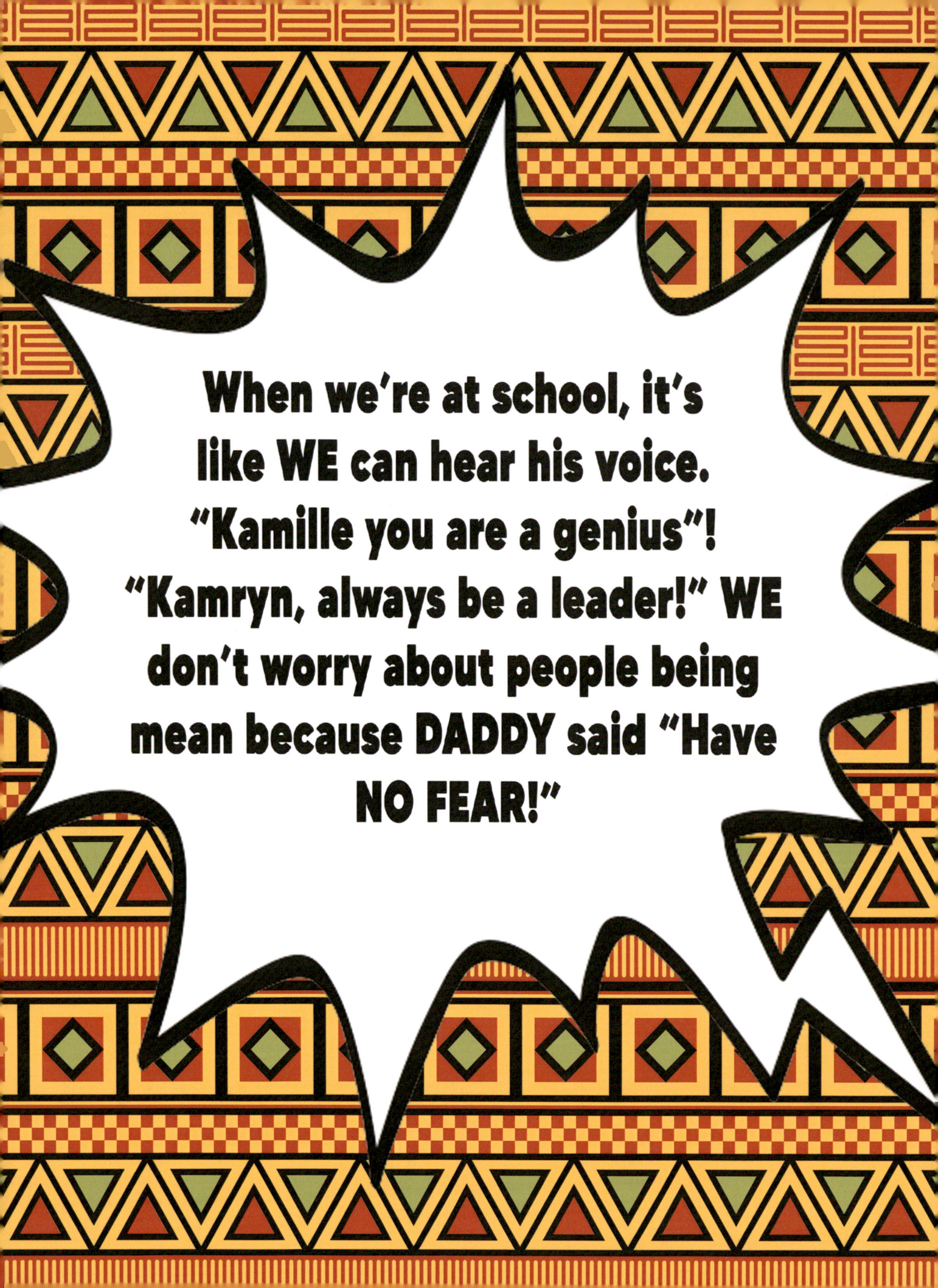

When we're at school, it's like WE can hear his voice. "Kamille you are a genius"! "Kamryn, always be a leader!" WE don't worry about people being mean because DADDY said "Have NO FEAR!"

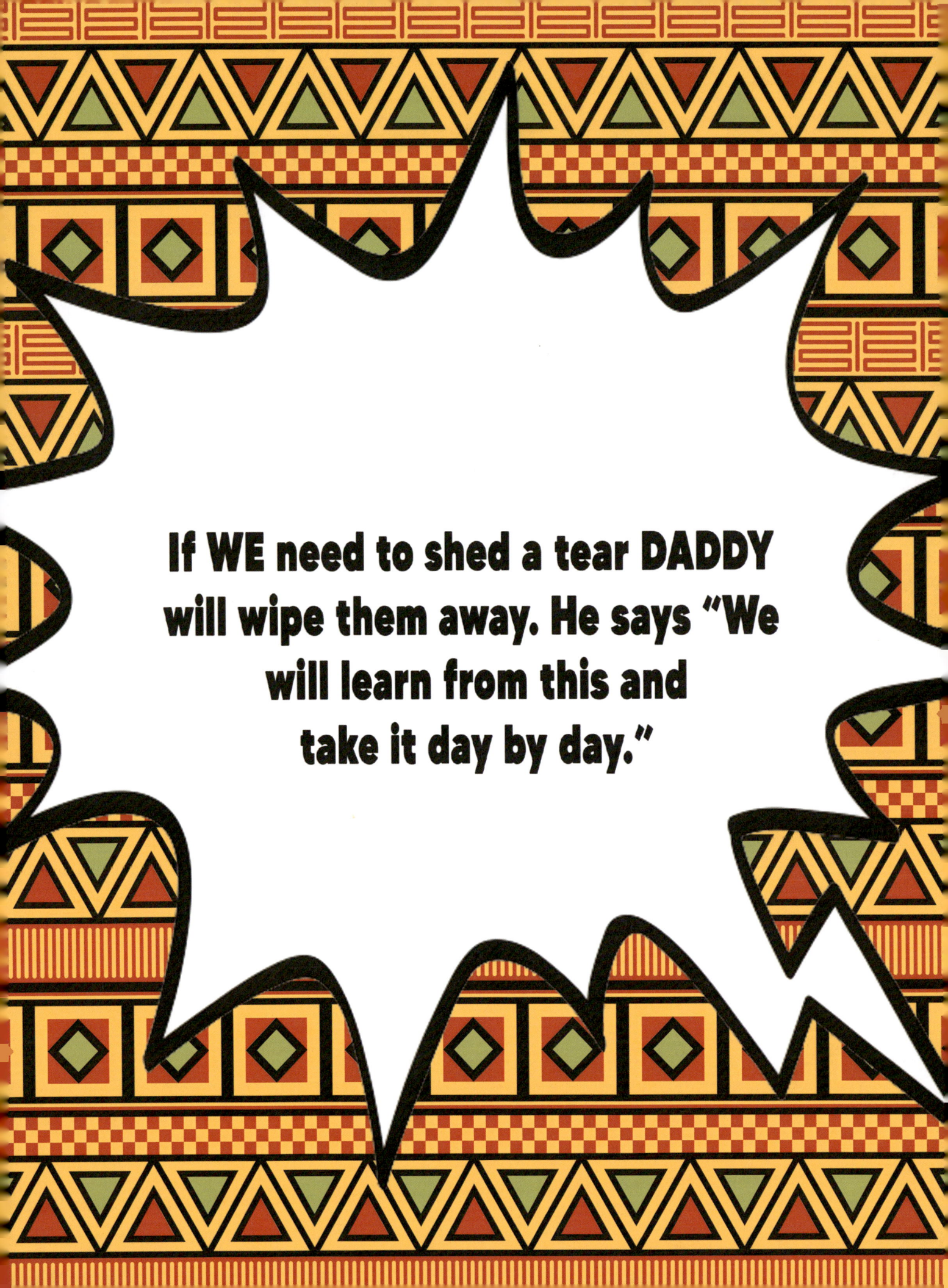

If WE need to shed a tear DADDY will wipe them away. He says "We will learn from this and take it day by day."

After school, we go to the gym and we love to play the games. The Rec Center is sooooo much fun, unless WE lose and feel the pain. DADDY says "don't be ashamed because when you lose, you gain."

Sometimes we do moves and sometimes we just shoot...BUT DADDY always says, "Have fun! This isn't war like ARMY troops!"

When we get home, it's time for dinner. Everytime WE leave the gym, WE feel like winners because DADDY tells us WE are. Mommy cooked salmon and green beans and, yes, WE love the yams.

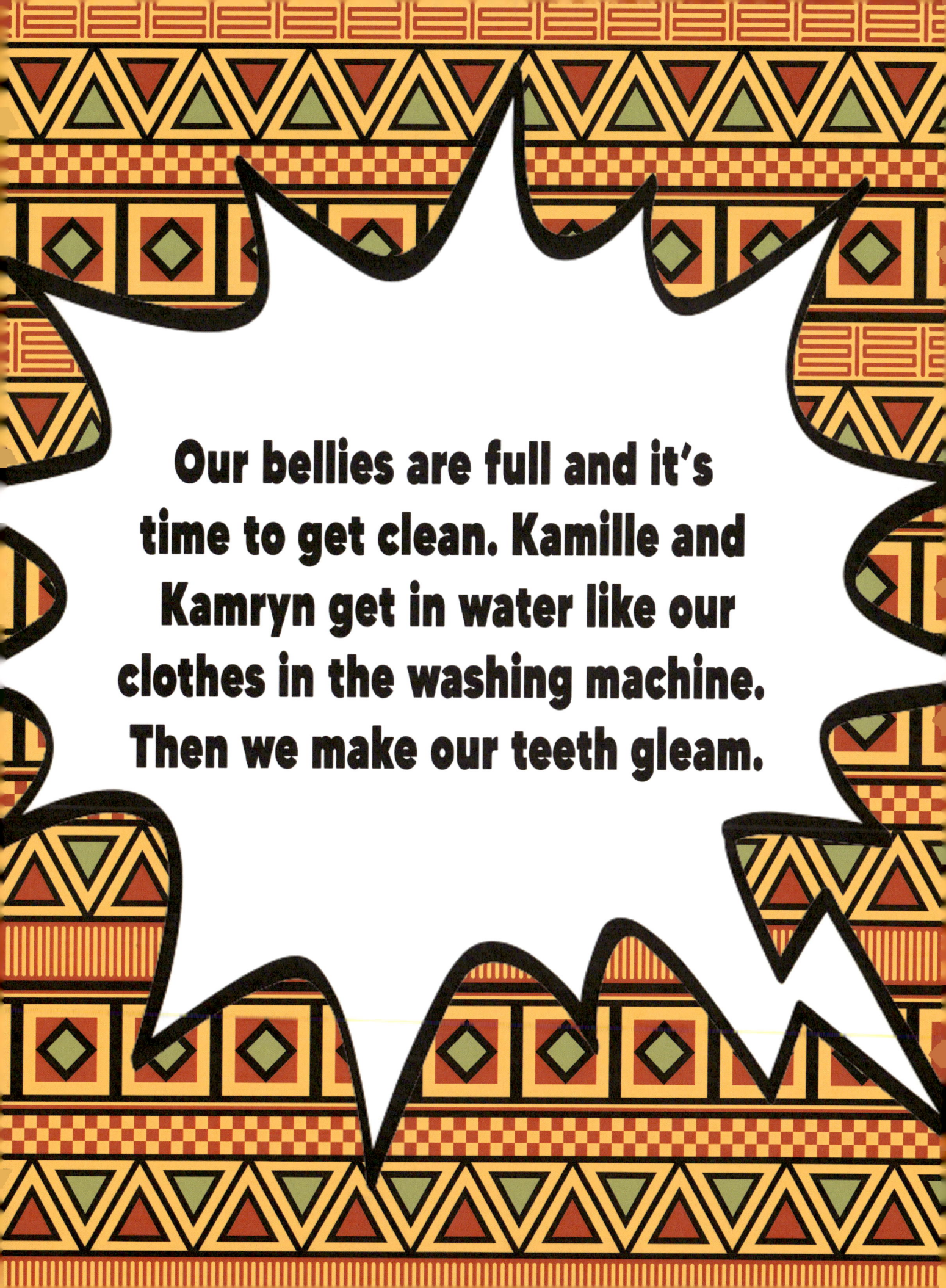

Our bellies are full and it's time to get clean. Kamille and Kamryn get in water like our clothes in the washing machine. Then we make our teeth gleam.

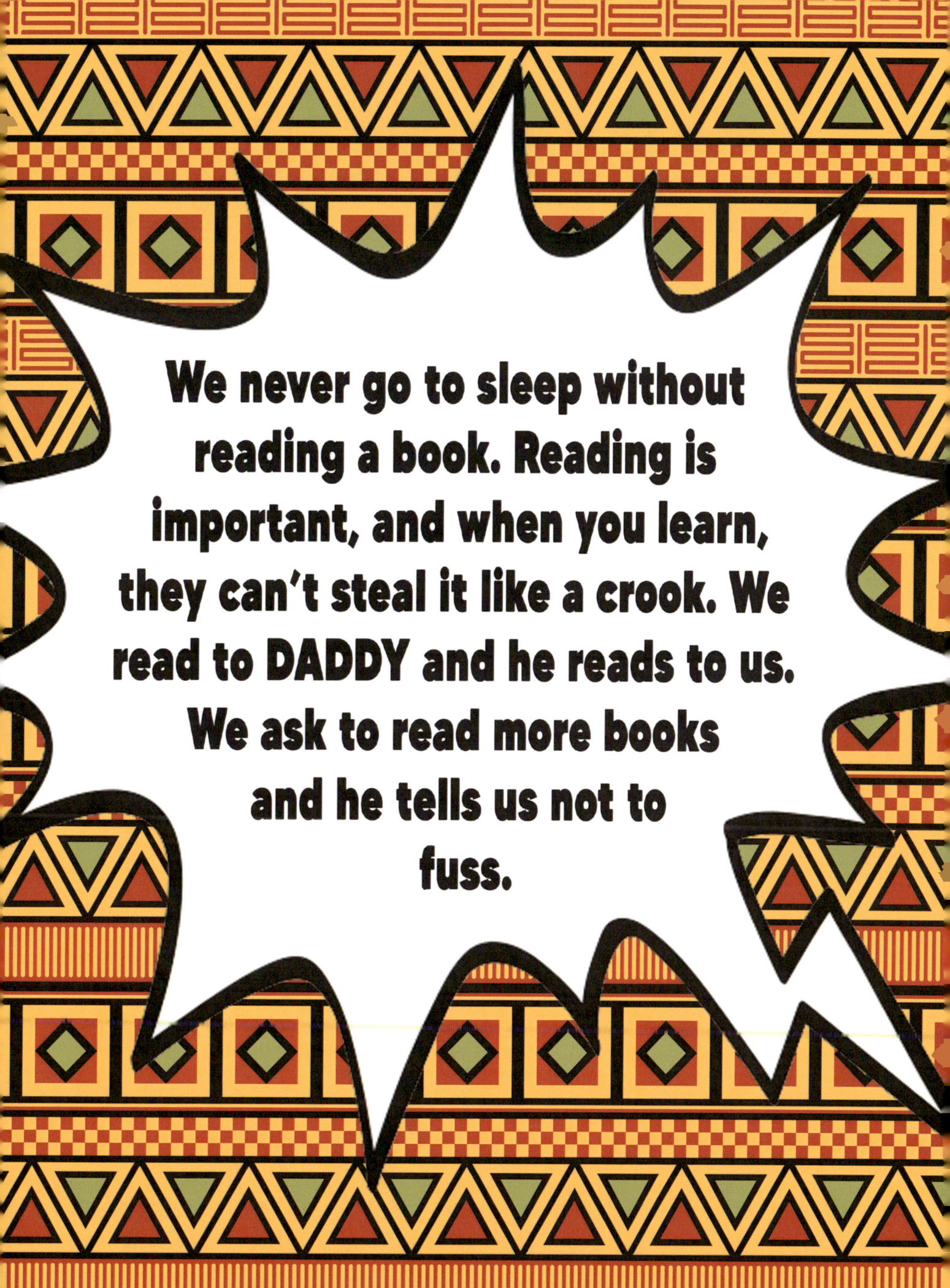

We never go to sleep without reading a book. Reading is important, and when you learn, they can't steal it like a crook. We read to DADDY and he reads to us. We ask to read more books and he tells us not to fuss.

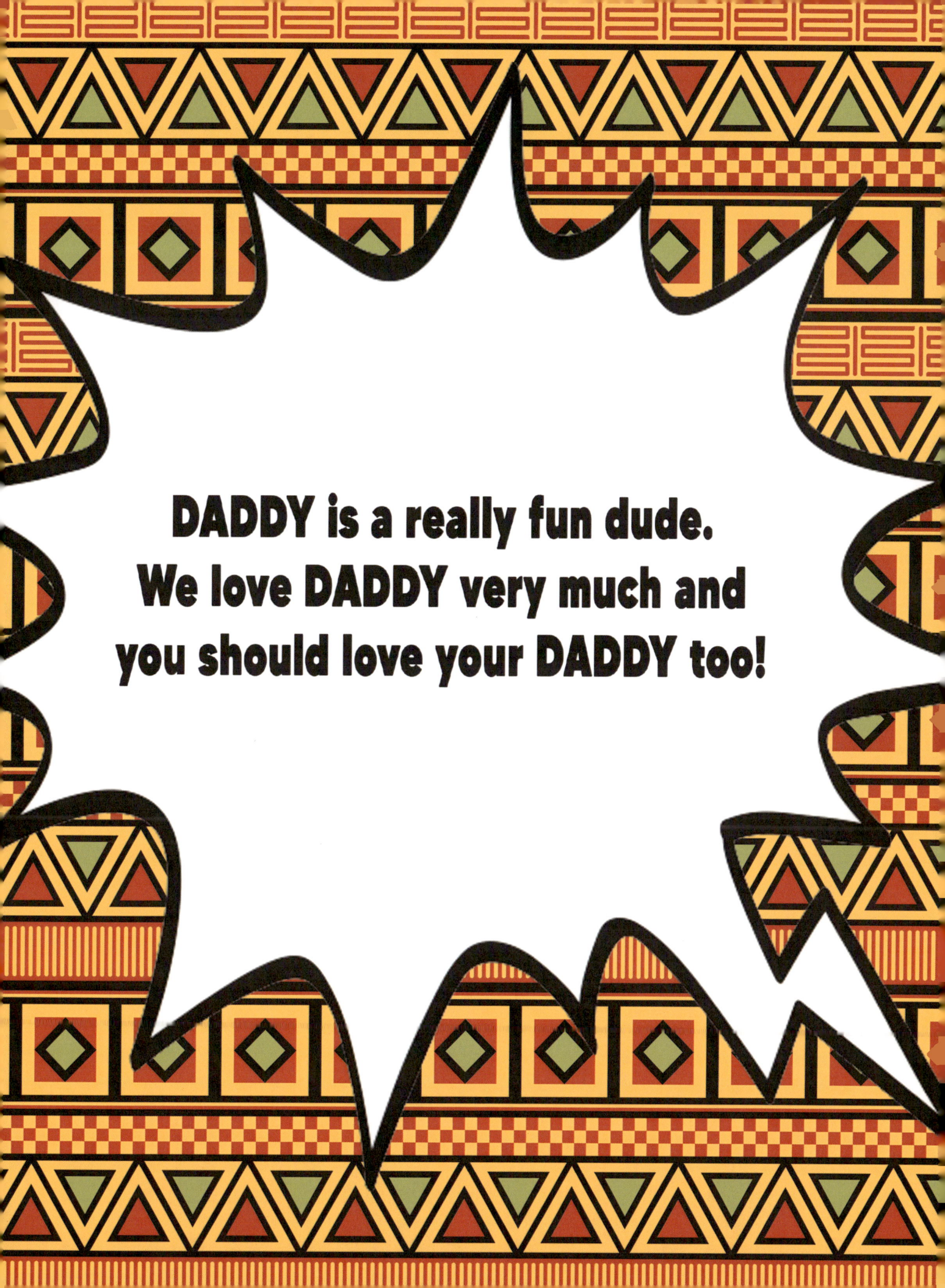

DADDY is a really fun dude. We love DADDY very much and you should love your DADDY too!

www.ingramcontent.com/pod-product-compliance
Lightning Source LLC
Chambersburg PA
CBRC091209010526
44107CB00022B/1266